BEN'S SEEDS

Thanks to Esra Elkadi for her support and advice
during the creation of each page of this book.

Special thanks to Maraya Loza Koxahn for
her great editorial advice.

BEN'S SEEDS

by
Bassel Elkadi

Ben always loved to read books about gardening. One day, after reading his favorite gardening book, he went to the shop to buy some seeds.

Ben was so happy to get his first seeds.
He said, "I have always wanted to grow
my own plants. It's time to do it now."

Ben got his shovel and dug a hole. He placed the seeds in the hole and covered them with soil.

Ben got his watering can and watered his little seeds. He hoped for a sunny day. He knew the next step was to wait with patience.

The next day, Ben went out to see if the seeds had sprouted. Instead, he saw two crows pecking at the dirt, trying to eat the seeds.

Ben yelled, "Go away crows, don't eat my seeds. I worked hard to plant them."

Ben read that building a scarecrow would help keep the crows away. So, he got some wooden sticks and old clothes and built a scarecrow to protect his seeds.

Ben gave the scarecrow his favorite hat and said, "I trust you scarecrow! Keep my seeds safe until they become huge plants and start blooming."

Every day that week, Ben went out to see if there were any sprouts.

One day, he even waited all afternoon, but there was nothing.

Ben went back to check his favorite gardening book to see if he had made any mistakes in the steps he had completed so far.

It was written that seeds need sunlight, a suitable temperature, nutrients in the soil, water, and air in order to sprout. It would take a week or more for them to show above the ground.

Ben didn't lose hope. He continued to care for his seeds daily.

Finally, a tiny green sprout poked through the earth. Ben felt so happy!

Ben waited for the other seeds to sprout too but, sadly, only one had survived.

Every day the sprout grew more,

and more ...

and more, until it became taller than Ben.

By the end of the summer, Ben's seed had turned into a big, green plant with beautiful yellow flowers. He felt so happy and proud of the result of his hard work and patience.

Ben took down his scarecrow and told him, "Thank you, for protecting my plant and its flowers, scarecrow.

We will have more seeds to plant together and protect from now on."

Made in the USA
Columbia, SC
30 May 2020